MUTUAL SHORES

Special thanks to: Scott Bade, Allegra Blake, Meggan Carney, Gabrielle Halko, Matthew Hollrah, Nancy Hall James, Alexander Long, Marianne Swierenga, and Bonnie Wozniak.

New Issues Poetry & Prose
The College of Arts and Sciences
Western Michigan University
Kalamazoo, Michigan 49008

An Inland Seas Poetry Book

Inland Seas poetry books are supported by a grant from The Michigan Council for Arts and Cultural Affairs.

First Edition, 2000.

ISBN: 0-932826-95-4 (paperbound)

Library of Congress Cataloging-in-Publication Data:
Sterling, Phillip
Mutual Shores/Phillip Sterling
Library of Congress Catalog Card Number (99-76774)

Art Direction:	Tricia Hennessy
Design:	Matt Siegrist
Production:	Paul Sizer The Design Center, Department of Art College of Fine Arts Western Michigan University
Printing:	Courier Corporation

MUTUAL SHORES

PHILLIP STERLING

New Issues

WESTERN MICHIGAN UNIVERSITY

for MRS A

Contents

III

Acknowledgements

Grateful acknowledgement is made to the editors of the publications in which these poems originally appeared:

Birmingham Poetry Review: "Give Us This Day"

The Georgia Review: "Heartsick"

The Kenyon Review: "Aesthetics," "Floridian Psychology," "Mating Season"

The Paris Review: "Mechanical Failure," "Pedestrian Tunnel to Clinch Park Zoo, Winter 1964," "Duplicate Scenes of the Earthly Paradise," "Behind the Cathedral, Liège," "The Isadora Duncan School, Berlin 1905"

Passages North: "North of Paradise"

Slant: "Cozumel"

Western Humanities Review: "Astronomy," "First Monday in September," "Color Tour," "'A Certain Slant'," "Roundelay," "Providence in the Fall of a Nuthatch," "Io in Florida," "The Widower Tells Other Passengers Where He's From"

"Duplicate Scenes of the Earthly Paradise" was reprinted in *1997 Anthology of Magazine Verse and Yearbook of American Poetry* (Monitor 1997).

I wish to thank Ferris State University and The Atlantic Center for the Arts for the generous support which enabled me to complete a number of these poems.

Nature is fine in love, and where 'tis fine
It sends some precious instance of itself
After the thing it loves.

—William Shakespeare, *Hamlet*

I

Aesthetics

Pleasure often comes like rain
waking us to certain coolness

unexpectedly on a humid
summer morning. We awaken

and our pleasure starts
to grow, not surprisingly

but with surprise, the way
crocuses or daffodils

shock us with rich color
against a canvas of late snow.

Or the way on summer's
hottest afternoon we dash

across the scorching dunes
toward cooler sand near shore

and come, quite accidently,
upon some stranger, who

removes a yellow bathing suit
completely, in full view.

How we're both embarrassed
and aroused! Rain at times

arrives like that, as pleasantly
as having someone catch

us by surprise—undressed,
unsmiling—and thinking

we're beautiful, raising
fragrances, balm and musk.

Astronomy

Missing the Blue
Light Special, insulted
by the not so youthful
young cashier, and fed
up having to return

a brand-new orange
plastic colander with
few unplugged holes,
we finally stormed out,
shortly before K-Mart

closed, to locate our car
in the lot. The night
was brutal, too warm
even for August.
Mosquitoes ravished us

at the door.
"Forget going anywhere
else," I said. "It's enough
if nothing worse happens!"
That's when

the lights went out.
Overloaded city-wide,
the power failed. Dozens
of consumers were
suddenly in the dark

and disoriented.
Then the sky
closed down on us
like a bank's computer,
and as never before

stars could be seen
by starless city dwellers.
"Wow!" came a child's
voice, which pretty
much summed it up

even for those who
couldn't speak. More
opinion followed:
"I know nothing about
stars—nothing at all—

but they seem so small!"
"Florida stars,"
someone heckled.
"They come here
for the summer."

Every so often this
happens, by chance,
or by circumstance
beyond our control:
we are astonished

by the obvious,
something astronomers
couldn't teach us
at school. "My daughter
once made a model

of the galaxy," said
a stranger, just before
our observatory closed.
"But it was really
nothing like this."

Tornado Drill

The first year we crouched beneath
our tiny desks, and it was enough,

especially for those in the lucky row—
those farthest from the vast windows

where the low clouds would first appear,
we were told, like a wild locomotive,

dark and fierce and unpredictable.
We hugged our knees until we ached

anxiously for the shatter of air
above our heads, the splash of safety

glass splaying across the classroom
like the April slush we'd stomped on

near the sidewalk at recess. My
socks, if I recall, were soaked.

The next year we'd been warned
in advance; the State required it.

We curled in the hall like gum wrappers
at the foot of our lockers, alphabetically

(should the need arise to identify
us, one from another), and we swooned

and giggled the whole time, imagined
how we must have looked to those who

assumed the truth: We'd die anyway.
Outside, the sky quizzed true or false;

one high cloud swept the outfield—its
last scribble of snow—like an eraser.

We practiced what we had learned.
We knew the sun would soon come to stay

and would draw from the gray rubble
at the playground's edge bright

snakes—how they'd rise there to bask,
unaware that the next brush of shadow

would be ours. We'd hide the slower
ones in our desks, anxious for the chance

to tease the kids we liked the best,
frighten those we didn't like at all.

Mechanical Failure

I'd just then turned away
from recording all the charge slips I'd laid
aside during morning rush—gas sales,
mostly, some donuts, coffee—
making up for the time I'd used
to refresh pots or fool

with cup dispensers, which
jam up fairly regular, most often
when traffic's tight—and since no car had
pulled in for a while, I thought
I'd get a break and maybe smoke
out back—that's when I heard

the awful wail of brakes,
the burning screech, and turning back around
I saw a brilliant blue Freightliner
run the intersection like
there's no tomorrow, jump the curb
and bear down for the pumps.

Oh my God! I thought. There's
nothing between me and *up in flames* but
glass and counterspace—the register,
one cellophane-wrapped yellow
rose, and a half-full plastic tub
of 5-cent bubble gum.

So what was I *supposed*
to think? I knew a woman once who'd lost
a child at birth—she said she'd never
be the same. And I knew then
if I survived, if for some saint's
mad purpose I was spared,

I'd feel such letdowns too—
at every high-pitched squeal, every kitten
mew, every desperate, metallic squawk—
and sure enough the truck just
grazed the number seven pump, stopped
short of snapping one and

five like matches. A sharp
smell of petroleum made my sore eyes
sear. You know, I left that job for good
that afternoon, and now I
just sell Avon on the side. I
guess I'll see my birthday

after all—no one is
forty-three very long. And you know,
the driver said that, bursting through
the door: "The whole works just up
and quit approaching 44!"
He'd been quite shaken too.

Shore Birds

Though near its end, the wounded gull
    still manages
to march along the modest beach
    between thick waves of dune grass and
        ambitious sand.

White head held up, white breast
    unbillowing, proud
as starch, he manages somehow to keep just
    out of reach, as children chase him
        down the beach.

A closer look confirms the worst.
    Exhausted, bleak,
he trails one wing like a broken gun,
    unchambered, ashen as gun-metal
        underneath;

it scrawls a message in the sand:
    Pity me,
and others in-between. At best, a gull's
    a scavenger, extorting bounty
        from discards,

who'll snatch tossed crusts of toast
    mid-air or
from an open hand pluck fishy, molded
    lumps of bread—at best, a comedy
        of flight,

a cartoon voice, an angel of spilled
    picnic barrels,
dumpsters, overwrought landfills. At worst,
    a gangster of Great Lake swill.
        At times we'd

chased them too, with a motorboat and
  baseball bat.
We'd caught small perch and fed one gull
  senseless, until, engorged, it no more
    flew than skipped

clumsily off waves, like some weighty,
  misshapen stone.
Then poised as for a curve-ball in the bow,
  we'd swung behind at top-speed and often
    come so close

we'd had to veer away, wiping spray
  and laughter
from our eyes. Eventually, the distance
  grew. Someone more merciful than I
    would likely take

a dinghy oar and kindly club this gull
  to death,
not leave its death to others of its kind;
  for I must side with those left behind,
    who seek their

livings from unforgiving shores. Let
  the children
play; I'll wait and watch the mourning
  dove poke about the fresh mulched
    lawn insectivorously—an

animated, random love—oblivious to her
    cousin's plight.
She'll spring from earth more easily,
    wings whistling familiarly the squeaks
        of summer's door.

North of Paradise

Whitefish Point, Michigan
—for Dorothy

One could learn to fly from a shore like this,
above a lake the size of Kansas,
where even in July winter is
a loon we can't see from the window,
a movement the eye rejects although
the ear admonishes it, like the last
yellow jacket of the season, perhaps,
or the yawn of a milkweed pod.

One could learn from timid sand how
even great lakes cower sometimes,
how anything is possible
when a multitude of waterfowl
takes wing from stubbles far from here,
launching into air (like souls)
shared songs of passage.

First Monday in September

The sun can rise without a prompt.
But I, prompted by the sun, have risen
earlier than I'd intended, dutifully,
to labor on the day declared labor-free
in celebration of summer's end.

I'm collecting from blackened sand
spent cartridges and fireworks scraps
we'd failed to find the night before
—before the wind corralled storm clouds
and blew up a flashy rodeo

more readily than our meager display
of rockets and Roman candles we'd
bought out-of-state, illegally.
A few were quite spectacular: they
popped and fizzed white brilliances,

or whistled, shrieked, even parachuted
green-glowing troopers to the beach,
where now I fill a Wal-Mart sack
with duds and other bits of Silver
Streaks, Gold Dusts, and Flying Jacks.

The other early signs of life
are isolated cirrus sheep
unloosed in bluest pastures to the west,
grazing with irreverence. That is,
until the morning duly breaks:

in two great leaps, two splashes
and a yip, the neighbor's waggish
coffee-colored labrador crashes
through the surface calm, shatters
the smooth, green-algaed foam

left from the late night revelry.
Forty yards offshore—at least—a yellow
plastic moon's afloat; and down the beach
a boy, leash in left hand, salutes
his right, then sights the fetch,

shouts, "Thor! Bring it back here!"
I've retrieved the worst of what I
think is ours—blunt nose cones, hard
cardboard hives, devil's cakes, Black Cat
packs—and still so much remains,

so many shreds and smatterings, so many
pulpy paper spores near the water's edge—
where Thor, well-praised, now
snorts and shakes, then lopes toward me
too casually. His tongue is proud.

But his wet, frothy, matted coat,
thick with sand and seaweed grit, smells
faintly, at first, of gasoline,
then reeks with the fishy stench
that's washed up onto shore.

Color Tour

The pink of steamed shrimp
or a sickly flamingo
may warn watchful sailors

of imminent storms, cold,
impending dangers, but on
this cool September

inland morning, pink
is a welcome color, worthy
of the white enameled,

dew-lapped, uncushioned
lawn chair on the deck.
Pink. Then yellow-pink,

orange-pink, pink
again, and back to white—
its tubing and taut straps

host levels of light, not
unlike the Bunsen flame
we'd poked with rods in

science lab, exploring
carbon's properties, or
stroked with vials lovingly,

while milk teeth dangled,
dissolved in carbonation.
Some colors must come

from chemical reaction,
chlorophyll, oxidation,
or a sunrise that weakens,

turns leaves full color,
and lets fall
filter through pale light,

paling to barely any light
at all, and leaving us
to lodge the chair

in a storage shed,
near garden tools, gas
grill and compost rake,

or watch it disappear
altogether, reduced
to real threats of snow.

Pedestrian Tunnel to Clinch Park Zoo, Winter 1964

Not the kiss alone
    but an essence of kiss,
its dark matter left undisclosed
by heavily clothed and insulated
bodies, the lips
    alone reckoning detail:

a questionable touch,
    the muffle of traffic and
slush, and the shy heart racing
across weakened ice disappears
like a snowmobile
    into depths of West Bay.

Only at memory's thaw
    will loss be found, paler,
older, though not so cold,
remarkably life-like, nudging
the impossible
    shore or loitering

against the snow fence
    near the entrance barred
for the season, hesitant at first,
then willing, even anxious,
to risk in awkward light
    a witnessed kiss.

The Blind Professor Waits for His Wife

Behind him, a nude male snow figure projects
a flagrant flamboyance into the courtyard of sororities,
remarking the wind. Its appearance bred conjecture: rude
and satyric, even bestial, the apparition would less
likely have risen on its own than been
modeled by an angry sophomoric beau, some unrequited

young stud swilled with tipsy vengeance and egged
on by a half-dozen beery, broken-hearted compatriots.
A drive-by sculpting, molded in likely defiance
of at least one sister's pristine, third-story
view, it was meant to personify—some believe—
the brutal, careless trampling of freshly fallen snow

—an honest, if not over-obvious, artifice.
The figure stands cocksure and cheeky, a sorry
Balzac of little more than its own strut.
The professor cannot see it, of course, knows
nothing of its artistry, and for the moment
cares even less for lovers' scufflings. He is

too cold; the snow does not appease him.
Of landscape, he knows this place; of weather,
its damp reproach and temperature as he waits
impatiently, statuesque and secure, a cane's full length
from the curb, his bare ears attuned to
the peculiar ticks and hum of an Oldsmobile

he's paid for but cannot drive. Unfamiliar with
sight's jittery adolescence—its readiness and raring to
go often insistent—he covets neither his neighbor's
wife nor swimsuit models, nor hungers near convenience
store magazines, where fleshy photos ache to come
alive. *Ignorance*—not blindness—*is bliss*, someone

has said. If truth be known, he too responds
to the post-coital perfumes of front row
co-eds, to the musk of cunt and douche,
and he too swirls with gendered abstractions, gags
on behavioral chants, and finds himself as shocked
by the flaccid sadness of winter's slow withdrawal

as by the figures that rise from snow
like braille, animating his darkest charts, and adding
to the statistical dance countless names of children
who stepped off curbs too early and vanished
from the visual world, who left behind mere
green and yellow flashes, warm bright-purple coats.

II

Duplicate Scenes of the Earthly Paradise

(18th century fireplace insert,
Musée de la Vie wallonne)

For the sake of argument pretend
we don't know who they are, this couple,
one on either side of a cast-iron tree
entwined with reptilian repose, dog-

faced, drooling. Obviously, the two are
not the same. On the right,
she confronts us, unashamed,
her not-quite-smile withheld to a smirk

in her pose, as if her model had meant
to shoulder innocence, all the while her flush
belying the artist's bed and not his brush.
The other's standing sidewise, from waist

down, more serious,
and yet his nub's a subtle
giveaway to the black gravity of his gaze,
a black apple in each hand.

Duplicate, but not identical,
molded in smokeless sheen
for some elaborate Walloon firepit:
on the right the tree takes hold of him,

enflames him, offshoots fired from his loins;
on the left the miscasting encircles her,
as though she bathes in rottled leaves
and fruit, molten earth, fecundity. Only

the serpent in both is the same, distracted
by the fragrance of apples in her hair
and heedless of the other side of the tree
wound in snakeskin.

"A Certain Slant"

"Over the centre of the North
doorway, we see a Virgin Mary;
the child has been destroyed."
—Guidebook to Notre-Dame de Paris

What there is to say about light
stained glass says. And what
there is to say about the saying
is often said in the translation
of saying, in the preliterate light
diffused by centuries of il-
lumination—by those who must withstand
both the light and its reformation,
the shuffling dust and thick-necked press
of tour groups in from the downpour,
mid-day, beneath the North Rose.

Here that smell is on us once again,
come round like a season, the smell
of tulips two weeks after bloom,
or some human smell, some sweat
diffused like light among the few who
come to worship where few still come
to offer thanks or confess, this thick press
moving as the light moves in spaces
insensitive to light, like red-blotched
Srebrenica snow or an orange tongue
licking Varsovia's golden wounds.

And bus after glistening bus unload
and unload into the mix, a communion of
breads turned flesh—wheat, white, rye, and gray—
an imitation of the world's *boulangerie*,
as if to say, "Isn't soda from the ashes
of plants and high-grade silica heated to fusion
beautiful! Aren't metallic oxides, iron and
copper, manganese and cobalt *beautiful!*
Isn't *grisaille* fired to black permanence
beautiful! Isn't molten paste blown to radiant
thicknesses, glazed in fragile radiance

beautiful!" As if to say, *Aren't we*
beautiful! Such an achievement of light!
—a monument to the long dead, to half-
carved gargoyles and unworked lead,
to the architects of light whose quick lives
weaken our knees at the sight. Such
an achievement of light!—a monument
to the recent dead, and to us, perspiring,
dizzy from incense and candle-heat,
half-conscious of our preparations not
for death but to make more dead,

to sanctify our alleluias, *our* cathedral tunes.
Among the press of tour groups, the whir
of Sony and Canon flash, beneath
the dimmest rose, mid-day, can we not see
open countryside, and wide, bright fields
of tulips, reds so brilliant our eyes ache
to take them in, an intense brevity of tulips?
—And are we not anxious then to move along,
break from the dim microbes of our scuffing along,
and re-enter the earthy smell of light rain
clipping its early wings on glass?

Behind the Cathedral, Liège

No one is willing to suggest
it's miraculous: the blood-like stain
weeping from the third of several
porcelain urinals
embedded in the stonework of St. Paul's;

that, shy of any deviltry,
there could be another venue of belief.
No man's been willing to enshrine it
and forgo
the practical amenities of pissing

in the open—to the relief
of lapsed parishoners, who obviously
don't mind when casual passersby
glance down
and greet them, heads and shoulders

rising from the level of
the street. No mystery here that men
relieve themselves; no miracle they
will pause
to pee. And as for those who must

believe in a body's privacy—
one's patience, strength, or modesty—
they'll find the solid wooden doors
that guard
a reliquary of Charles the Bold

are left unlocked, and expect
to be, in fact have warped, and never
closed completely since the last and
final occupation
of the last and final war.

The Isadora Duncan School, Berlin 1905

By the fifth day of rain
a few had begun to dance,
though not quite properly,
never having danced before.
Some swayed in corners;
others tapped leather heels
descending marble stairs.
One pair moved imperceptibly
through the garden, the way
humidity dulls a field where
hay bales graze like deer.
The rest could barely imagine
what they knew:

that the dance must rise
from danceless depths like
a trout, must leap and loose
the tugs of breathless
resignation; that our thin
tunics must by nature reveal,
and our bright scarves trail
dangerously, snapping and
whipping wicked air, taunting
wind with gravity; that
coming to light on small,
unshod feet, uninjured, may
be all we know of grace.

Give Us This Day

fête de saint nicolas, Liège

When we ask, as we must, what it means
to wander in white habit upon the hill
just at evening, herding in the motley cows
that graze the ancient Carmelite cemetery,
overwild since the war, calling their names
like vespers, shall the answer take the form
of prayer, or don a soiled lab-coat
and come begging, like students hustling
in the name of St. Nicolas, money for beer?

Often what's expected is more dreadful
than what is. For hours on a winter's eve
we'd stared at taut thin strings of light
where the hefty curtains scarcely closed,
afraid to cross the room and look below,
where gendarmes in dark riot gear
blazed nightsticks much more randomly
than common sense thought possible. And
to say it shouldn't happen here is not

much help, or that the students mean
no harm, their lame wings molting. We'll give—
or say we've given already—and hope
it's enough for them to hear "I'm sorry"
or "I gave," enough to overcome their urge
to mark us with stark flour or an egg
caught like graffiti on the back of dry-
cleaned overcoats, the ritual of some religion
they no longer understand.

So we grasp our children's hands to pass,
or briefly stop and watch *Le Navigateur*
barge beneath tinged cherubs, pursue its
load of early Ardennes snow down river,
heralded by an evergreen on the red-lit bow
just now passing the businessman
whose car shows signs that he refused.
Already warm with drink, these pseudo-
surgeons operate to spread an open wound.

But they ignore us, all the same. As if
we'd just stepped out to fetch the cows
from browsing among graves, robed
as white as the litanies we hum
while all the modern world goes whizzing by.
As if respect is owed to us, or to our
Grand Saint Nicolas, returning
joy from salt pork barrels, and gifts,
and days when we'd no longer have to beg.

Once home we kneel, unknot, remove
our children's shoes at the carpet's edge,
where it's come apart. And say: *Relax,*
It's over now, No harm's been done.
Tomorrow, or not so far beyond, we'll laugh
at spilled cake flour as we bake a child's
birthday treat and not smell fear in it,
nor feel we'd have to give back thanks
for the bread we've purchased daily.

Heartsick

You used the word first
as words are first used,
thinning suggestion from unutterable
air, and then we were both
stuck for something to say
and merging to a kind of *bouchon*,

a line of tour buses backed up
as far as a person could see,
doubling under the overpass,
with the delay interminable—
so much so the tongue swells
at the thought of speaking

angrily about it.
It's the same no matter what
clock notches ticks into us:
someone's coming into rapture,
or someone's leaving it, or
someone having left it already

awaits someone else's meager
acclaim, impatient to be
disposed of at last and in
from the sun. Someone lurches,
and someone stalls,
and someone's left behind.

For the heart is irreducible.
And the sickness of a heart
is barely remissive, boring
its mealy way beneath the outer
bark and depositing there
a million eggs or more,

larvae of some repulsed desire,
expectation's delirious sap.
There are times when the body
splays and flares, dizzy with thin-
winged annoyances, clogging
our nostrils and buzzing our ears

to deafness. And there are times
with nothing left to say
when we ache to say anything,
or fiddle with our feeble radio
and wonder when—if ever—
we'll be on the way again.

In My Anger Your Touch

In my anger your touch
is that of a washerwoman
soaping crooked paving stones
down a cold and narrow one-way
street each morning, as her
mother did, her mother's mother.
The bucket steams as we go by,
hurriedly, on our way to school,
salon lavoir, grocery store,
—anywhere, as long as we've
passed before she squeegees
to the curb dogshit and lye.
Every day the same.

Every day the same:
something in the way we rise
to night's deposits, riverdrift,
rain's remains, the crumpled,
peeling odds or bitter ends of
what, in time, may taint love
loves us just the same.
At the corner you turn
half-way to glance at where
she bends, her apron laughs.
Then take my hand.
Every place must have its god
and here is no different.

The Saint of Wisps, Perhaps

And the sabbath rang slowly
In the pebbles of the holy streams.
—Dylan Thomas

When the name of someone who loved us once
startles us to reminiscence—like sudden
rain against a gray, third-story window
that overlooks the ashen chimneys of unlit
Liège rooftops, amber street lamps,
a red car idling at the curb—we know
it's Sunday. We can tell by the wind.

Such moments have a patron saint too:
the thin ties of businessmen glint
and flit like underwings above the *Champs*
des oiseaux, flock at the docked silver
sheen of hand-pressed suit pants,
whirl against October's overwashed wool
sky. The only other flight's a brace

of children's pale legs, earthly in
their games and play;—as is my son,
backed up before a wall chalked square
with penalties, his tartan scarf taut
as an acolyte, who prepares himself
for the worthy launch of a stunning world,
grimacing at its iron song.

Come on, I say. *Ça va? Okay?*
It's just the train to Louvain.

We'd dined quite well, a Sunday's meal,
then rested; and at our leisure hiked
the heights of listless hills, to the fiercer
winds of the playground, from where, before
our match, we'd watched the river move,
marked by pallid garbage sacks that glare
like women's legs in storefronts near

the station, office chairs adjusted to
their different lengths of leg; the floodlit
harmonious windows at which, passing in
the bus just then we'd have heard someone
murmur, "I wonder if they're friends."
Or count how many chairs stand empty,
as if the wind had caught them unaware.

Tomorrow she'll return to
turning back foreskin in her oiled lap,
or the swatch of delicate Belgian lace
she crimped at mass the day
the first small colonies of blood
appeared. But for today, she'll
merely stop to watch a father and son

prepare to shoot some goals a dark
and breathless autumn afternoon.
Keep your center low!
His eyebrows pinch the rain.
Ça va? Okay?
How long
their warm breath plays upon the air!

How brief the moment renders its
remembrance:
The rain invokes
no patron saint—no scuffed,
deflating soccer ball, no birds, no
foreign pipework, no red car,
no women idling in windows

(heads bowed,
filing their nails incessantly),
no paper pulse, no glue of vanity
—only in this thin house long asleep
a restless, solitary heartbeat;
and at the window, wind:
the name of one someone once loved.

Epiphany: *Galette du Roi*

As if one didn't know
  already; as if our sweet cake
    had no bean, and one
no sovereign chance to be;

As if no silver paperboard
  could foil master's crown,
    no teethed bitch snarl
at master's lively call;

As if some wish for New
  Year's snow is more than
    half its handsome masquerade,
its foolish frenzy—

Serve me first. And let me
  be the one to choose
    in my ardor all this
day's glory, and its song.

A Former Belgian Emissary Speaks of the Solace in Marriage

The familiar doesn't have to breed
sameness. Consider, for instance,
the place on the body I've come to call
frangipani—for its fragrance,
its unsettling, nameless colors—
and not for any resemblance to
some cobbled, ill-illumined alley
near the Grand' Place,

where darkness gives way only
to the well-tippled or incautious;
or The Academy of Fools,
whose juggling antics beg and coddle
jet-lagged tourists with amusement,
leaving daylight to the dreary supplicants
who colonize the shopworn
storefronts of St. Nicholas.

It's a place where language
mounts no meager stage, no distant,
incoordinate rebellion, no scar
or Stanleyville of youthful exuberance
—just a strange sweet taste
of the ever unfamiliar, like *moules*
and yeasty beer; equal in sustenance
to bread. It's the love

of the steadfast, the spirit
engendering flesh, the *you and me*:
missionaries in a jungle of fortune,
where every unnamable lust grows
cultivated and domestic, and rises
with indiscriminate brightness
from all that is loathsome
or poisonous, or inhospitable.

III

Roundelay

They lived happily for many years
in what could have been a small
pastel house near the airport

where egrets, those yellow-footed
spirits, littered the safety zone
like a newspaper blown from a porch

in what could have been a small
disaster, litter lifted into props
like a newspaper blown from a porch

where spirits, those yellow-footed
egrets, happen to call early one
radiant Sunday morning and lift

from what could have been a small
pastel house near the airport, where
litter from the safety zone lifts

into air like egrets early one
radiant Sunday morning, the happiness
they'd lived with for many years.

Floridian Psychology

The leaves are full of chameleons,
licks of lanky arabesques that leap
from leaf to palm, or drop from eaves,
raining from unguttered roofs.
Shooting in short bursts of speed
down the gray-green bark

of twisted trees, they zip from color
to color, nearly camouflaged.
Not the least attractive of reptilia,
some have been known to house
in aquariums complacently and
entertain bored school-children

during winter storms. They thrive,
however, in luscious, unspoiled
cover of subtropical vegetation, well-
suited to the backwashes of Florida.
Agile, deceptive, swift—one may note
an uncanny likeness to the id.

The ego, on the other hand, is clumsy,
lugged from one place to another
like suitcases of winter clothes or cellos
on public transportation—or rather
like the slow, endangered manatees,
blubber-faced clowns of warm tidal

river basins, locked in to near-
extinction by pleasure-seeking power
boats. One sees them periodically,
lost in blatant paradise, heads surface-
mined and humps full-scarred,
"old bowling balls with eyes, but not

so bright," just below the surface
of the estuary, nudging with primordial
care each other, or some harmless
human swimmer—a careless,
unassuming adolescent, suffering to be
both loved and left alone.

Sight Reading

New Smyrna Beach, Florida

My young friend, a sculptor, is losing
her hair. She tells me the fine matting
clogs her bathroom sink and that nothing
can be done about it, according

to her doctor, who should know.
At first, we both treated it as a joke.
"You'll look like alabaster," I said, "after
it's polished!" She saved clumps of hair

in a bag. And when the bag grew thick,
she spun and wove the hair into a tapestry
with other things—moss, palm leaves,
cord grass, mangrove sticks—

and hung it in the air to dry.
I can see the work from my upper window
and I admire it very much, although
it's somewhat abstract. Only by

looking hard have I been able to discover
some geography—some tidal estuary,
like Turnbull Bay—something like a photo
taken for reconnaissance, farther away

than my beautiful, pale friend could ever go.
Now it's quite clear, the figure so obvious
there's no mistaking it any longer—
a small, dark scar, dim on heaven's penis.

Providence in the Fall of a Nuthatch

By midday the patio
is raucous with mourners.
Along the rail, doves
like plump widows coo
and carry on, call me
to the back door, where
a small black feather

clings to thermalpane.

The ceremony is brief:
a high lob into brush
beyond our common fence
where an unwelcome cat
is known to prowl. Birds
and the beasts of field
adore me.

I Saw in Louisiana Walt Whitman

One could always be mistaken, of course,
mis-visioned by the desire for fame, or wealth,
or notoriety—but then, who wouldn't want to turn

to one's companion, poking through the Milky
Way's and Juicy Fruit's, the *Self's*, the *Cosmo's*
—pinch them by the sleeve, and say (in feigned

astonishment, of course, the *public* voice):
"Well, lookee here! I told you so!"
Who wouldn't want to own a dozen copies

of a front-page (slightly retouched) photo
of you and Walt—lusty, rude—two
"PALS OF POETRY," his manly, compassionate arm

across your shoulder in open, honest affection,
not *affected* fondness. See! His beard can't hide
the slight, though obvious, grin.

—And yet, I suppose, one could be mistaken.
Friendships don't always turn out friendly.
Some may, in fact, *prefer* a leafy, moss-twined

souvenir—shelved with others of its kind—
to living flesh. Good hygiene's not a guarantee;
history's so often questionable.

And there may be other, well, *predilections*
one cannot abide. Friends may well arrive
with many heavy loads of extra baggage.

So I saw in Louisiana Walt Whitman, standing
near the road—rude and lusty, unbending,
alone—in a field cropped miserably low,

and as I sped along, my windows powered up
and the air on high, conscious of my destination,
conscious of the time,

I considered pulling to the side and offering
my assistance, as he'd have done for me.
But I knew very well I would not.

Io in Florida

The cows of Volusia County
would not choose to stay
here, beneath thin shades
of palm and slash pine.

Nor are they sacred.
Nor will they be spared.
They live out their days
as if awaiting lovers.

The cows are beautiful,
sad. They wear their long
faces like sarcophagi.

On cloudless nights
a hundred eyes—and more—
guard their simple lives.

Mating Season

Spring enters warmer climates
like a student in the wrong
classroom. It wants to leave
quickly, yet for some inexplicable
reason, stays and pretends
to be autumn. Small, dry leaves,
brown as the empty casings of
palmetto bugs, worry the paths,
scurry at the first whisk of wind.
Ground-cover routs growth.
Trees remain unswayed.

Only a small green lizard
offers hope. Leaving the drab
undergrowth for a branch of wild
blueberry, he struts, cocks his
head to the sun, bobs three times,
puffs out his neck, and displays
his intent, as red as the flesh
of a blood orange. He is proud
of his achievement! Only
with a little arrogance may one
find some things acceptable.

Cozumel

> *"The sigh of History rises over ruins,*
> *not over landscapes . . ."*
> *—Derek Walcott*

We can get no closer than
thick scrub brush and
lush palmetto that overrun
the trenched cut called
a road (which we'd been
told was impassable
to begin with) and so
maneuver the leased Jeep

around a clay-sharded
swatch wide enough for it,
heading back to the newly
thatched cabanas of our
expansive resort, where
cool, pink, rum-slumbered
drinks are waiting for us,
already paid for. We

lack the grit of Mayans,
it seems, who slashed
the first paths to sacred
ground and slaved stone
temples into being there,
emblazoned civilization—
or even of these Cozumelenos
whose thin, dust-slacked

dogs loll in the rutty,
washed-out road, where we
slow, attentively, to pass
the yawning stables or
petty domiciles decked
with gods, Aztec calendars,
bright-edged birds and fish,
brandishing trademarks—

hand-loomed rugs of wool,
cotton, polyester blends.
Not until the pavement
begins do we pull in and
stop, drawn at last to
a squat-walled, time-pocked
shop—one of few and far
between that advertise:

Cold Beer, Souvenirs, Dive
Trips, VISA. Here we can
hold the family pet, an
ancient iguana, "for nothing"
—though warned not to put
our faces too near—then tip
the owner dollars (at *his*
insistence) for a photo.

The monkey, Señor, will
do tricks too! But we've
caught on already; we'll
ask for nothing more
than directions to the fuel
station in San Miguel—
the only one, we're told,
on the island. We're

anxious now to get back
and change, go snorkeling,
sightsee Palancar reef, or
lounge in the pool beside
the bar, lingering in sun,
fingering ice-laden drinks
and snacking to our heart's
content on pineapple and

melon, tortillas, guacamole—
spoiling our supper, perhaps,
but getting our money's
worth. What we don't eat
we'll feed to the great-tailed
grackles on the beach.
The ruins we didn't see
will be there another day.

The Widower Tells Other Passengers Where He's From

Here,—the hand's a lesson in geography,
the right palm facing, or the backside
of the left, forested with pine-like
follicles along knuckled hills and shore-
line, veined with purple interstates.

Notice in particular the extremities:
thumb callused by the hard-held farm, blunt
and bruise-ruddied as a sugar beet; or
the wounds and healings, the jagged scars
our lumbered dunes have scoured.

—For the hand will occasionally reach
into mistaken places—pause dangerously
in dreamy reminiscence—or grasp at
reckless situations like perch dorsals.
How we envy the other cousin, little

finger nuzzled by the local myth of
a sleeping bear, whose cubs will surely
follow her to shore! *So much of any place,*
she'd said, *is pain*—or being left
in place, the place from where it spreads.

Out of place we know where we belong; we
thrust our sufferable selves like peninsulas.
And though our roads are paved with foreign
gravel, asphalt, or cobblestones (even
the sandy loam of late geologies), one hand

may prod and pare another's fingernails,
or twiddle thumbs, or sculpt peaked
steeples out of prayer. Another may hold
its brief applause. The weather too
is often found more tolerable than welcome.

Memorial Day

The beach is dead.
Its towels, chairs, umbrellas
have been packed away
or carted home,
stowed until the next holiday.
Even the *Cold Drinks* man
with the bleached ponytail
has shuttered his blue van
and is gone. The sky is gray.
A single cloud stretches
like canvas overhead.

I'm straddling my bike,
having just now stopped
near the paint-flaked railing
of an access ramp
closed to motoring
for the night. As far
as I can see, the only
others left on the beach are
two small girls poking
at something in the outgoing tide.
And the only sound, like

terns in the air
above bagel scraps, is laughter
swooping from the open
porch of a faded pink bar.
What I love about the ocean
is how empty it can appear;
and yet, how day after day
it will muster
strength for undulation
—some days dangerously so—
and how there

beneath those waves,
within the churning
undercurrent, life can
evolve with an intensity unsettling
to those of us bound by land.
So these are my options: I
could be unfaithful.
I could chain my
bike to the No Parking
sign by the Beachcomber Bar and
drink until I crave

the start
of something ending,
an unfamiliar body
in a stranger's bed.
Or I could simply ride away,
my pedal's tiresome squeaking
rhythmic as a heart.
Or by walking
down another way,
I could swim
until it's dark.

photo by Rachel Sterling

Phillip Sterling was born in Michigan and raised along its lakes. While his education and employment have for periods of time located him to other shores, since 1987, when he joined the faculty at Ferris State University, he has considered Big Rapids, Michigan, his primary residence. Among his awards are a National Endowment for the Arts Fellowship in Poetry, a PEN Syndicated Fiction Award, a Distinguished Faculty Award from the Michigan Association of Governing Boards, and two Senior Fulbright lectureships (Belgium and Poland). His poems, stories, and essays have appeared in many periodicals, both here and abroad, including *The Paris Review*, *The Kenyon Review*, *The Georgia Review*, *Western Humanities Review*, and *AWP Chronicle*. *Mutual Shores* is his first collection.

New Issues Poetry & Prose

Editor, Herbert Scott

James Armstrong, *Monument in a Summer Hat*
Anthony Butts, *Fifth Season*
Gladys Cardiff, *A Bare Unpainted Table*
Lisa Fishman, *The Deep Heart's Core Is a Suitcase*
Joseph Featherstone, *Brace's Cove*
Robert Grunst, *The Smallest Bird in North America*
Edward Haworth Hoeppner, *Rain Through High Windows*
Josie Kearns, *New Numbers*
Lance Larsen, *Erasable Walls*
David Dodd Lee, *Downsides of Fish Culture*
Deanne Lundin, *The Ginseng Hunter's Notebook*
Joy Manesiotis, *They Sing to Her Bones*
David Marlatt, *A Hog Slaughtering Woman*
Paula McLain, *Less of Her*
Malena Mörling, *Ocean Avenue*
Julie Moulds, *The Woman With a Cubed Head*
Marsha de la O, *Black Hope*
C. Mikal Oness, *Water Becomes Bone*
Margaret Rabb, *Granite Dives*
Rebecca Reynolds, *Daughter of the Hangnail*
Martha Rhodes, *Perfect Disappearance*
John Rybicki, *Traveling at High Speeds*
Mark Scott, *Tactile Values*
Diane Seuss-Brakeman, *It Blows You Hollow*
Marc Sheehan, *Greatest Hits*
Phillip Sterling, *Mutual Shores*
Angela Sorby, *Distance Learning*
Russell Thorburn, *Approximate Desire*
Robert VanderMolen, *Breath*
Martin Walls, *Small Human Detail in Care of National Trust*
Patricia Jabbeh Wesley, *Before the Palm Could Bloom: Poems of Africa*